9163 Br.

D0538573

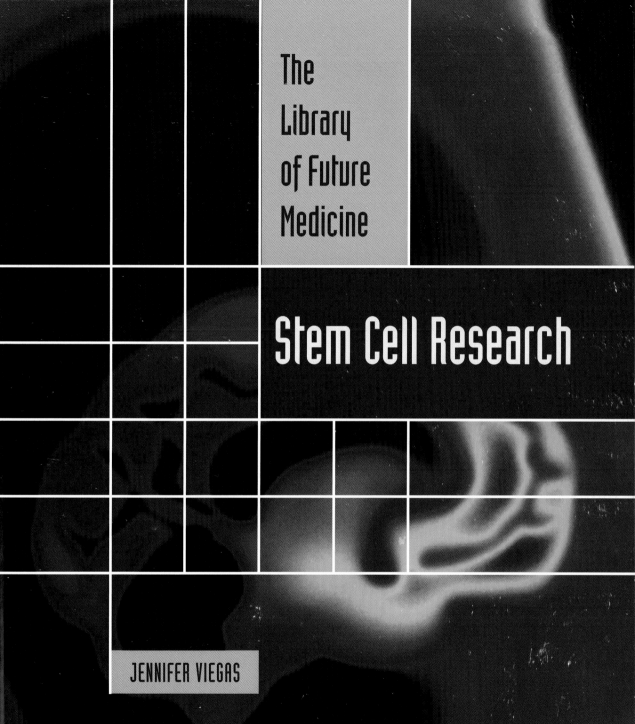

# The
# Library
# of Future
# Medicine

# Stem Cell Research

JENNIFER VIEGAS

The Rosen Publishing Group, Inc.
New York

Published in 2003 by The Rosen Publishing Group, Inc.
29 East 21st Street, New York, NY 10010

**Library of Congress Cataloging-in-Publication Data**
Viegas, Jennifer.
Stem cell research / Jennifer Viegas.— 1st ed.
p. cm. — (The library of future medicine)
Includes bibliographical references and index.
Summary: Discusses the latest scientific breakthroughs regarding embryonic stem cells and the growing of new human tissues, and how this can help doctors treat human illnesses.
ISBN 0-8239-3669-4
1. Stem cells—Juvenile literature. 2. Embryonic stem cells—Juvenile literature.
[1. Stem cells. 2. Cells. 3. Medicine.] I. Title. II. Series.
QH587 .V54 2002
616—dc21

2001006263

*Manufactured in the United States of America*

**Cover image:** Colored scanning electron micrograph of an eight-cell embryo, three days after fertilization.

# Contents

Human epithelium cells growing in an artificial culture. Scientists hope to grow stem cells and transform them into specialized tissues in the same way.

# Introduction

Scientists are working on research that could one day dramatically improve your life, along with the lives of every other person in the world. Imagine never having to worry about many of the effects associated with certain diseases, disabling injuries, and aging. At present, magical cures usually happen only in movies and science fiction novels. Stem cell research, however, may transform science fiction fantasies into life-saving realities.

Considering how important they may be, stem cells are very tiny things. Stem cells are not visible to the naked eye. They can be seen under a microscope only after being stained with a fluorescent, or glowing, dye and after undergoing magnification anywhere from twenty to forty times. Stem cells resemble miniature soap bubbles bunched up together, but looks can be deceiving. These small cells, in the not-so-distant future, could cure many deadly diseases, such as diabetes, cancer, heart disease, and Alzheimer's. Several scientists even believe that stem cells may one day provide the key to human immortality.

A typical animal cell. The large circular object is the nucleus. To the left of the nucleus (the small blue oval) is a mitochondrion. Mitochondria provide cells with energy. The small dots are ribosomes, where proteins are made.

# 1 ▷ A Cell Primer

All cells have certain attributes in common. For example, they all are constructed in a similar way. Each human cell consists of an outside wall, or membrane. This membrane is porous and semipermeable. This means that while it provides a barrier around the cell, similar to a balloon filled with water, it also can allow other substances, such as oxygen and nutrients, to pass through it, the way a sponge can soak up water.

While cells work together in the body's systems, each individual cell functions like a separate living organism. A cell needs food for energy and building materials, and oxygen and water to survive. That is why it is important for the membrane around the cell to be porous, so that the cell may interact with its environment. Because we are made of cells, the same is true for us. We need to eat food, breathe oxygen, and drink water. Like cells, we also have to be able to get rid of waste material, such as when we exhale carbon dioxide, a waste product of cellular metabolism.

When cells are inside the body, however, they pretty much take care of themselves. We do not have to devote attention to each and every cell, which is a good thing. It would be like caring for millions of pets each day! One reason that cells work so efficiently is that their structure has many things in common with other parts of the human body. For example, we have organs that perform necessary functions. These organs include the heart, which pumps blood, the lungs, which breathe in air, and the kidneys, which filter waste material out of bodily fluids. Cells also have tiny organs, called organelles, that perform similar tasks within each individual cell.

# ORGANELLES

The organelles are suspended in a runny, jellylike substance called the cytoplasm. The cytoplasm is between 70 and 80 percent water. Its texture is similar to Jell-O, which allows the cytoplasm to hold the organelles in place. The placement of the organelles is comparable to the way pieces of fruit may be suspended within Jell-O.

Four types of organelles within the cytoplasm are mitochondria, ribosomes, lysosomes, and the Golgi apparatus. Under a microscope, mitochondria look like small, cylindrical tubes. Enzymes, or complex proteins that cause chemical reactions to take place, act on the mitochondria, directing them to convert oxygen and nutrients into energy that the cell can use.

Ribosomes help to make protein for the cell and are associated with the production of ribonucleic acid, a substance that is involved in the transmission of inherited genetic characteristics such as hair color, eye color, and height. Ribosomes also make substances that are used when cells need to repair themselves. Lysosomes resemble tiny eggs. They contain enzymes that help the cell use the energy produced by the mitochondria. The several minute organelles that make up the Golgi apparatus store substances necessary to bodily function, such as hormones. Hormones are chemical messengers that trigger specific responses in other organs.

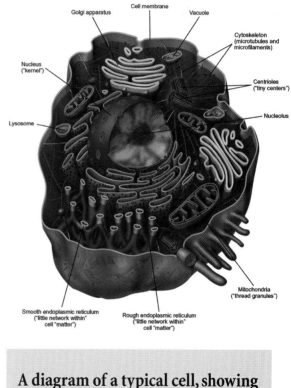

Golgi apparatus    Cell membrane    Vacuole

Cytoskeleton (microtubules and microfilaments)

Nucleus ("kernel")

Centrioles ("tiny centers")

Lysosome

Nucleolus

Mitochondria ("thread granules")

Smooth endoplasmic reticulum ("little network within" cell "matter")

Rough endoplasmic reticulum ("little network within" cell "matter")

A diagram of a typical cell, showing the nucleus and various organelles

# THE NUCLEUS

At the center of most cells is a nucleus, another organelle separated from the rest of the cell by its own membrane. The nucleus is a very important part of the cell because it contains the genetic information that programs many human characteristics. That information is stored in a chemical called deoxyribonucleic acid, or DNA for short.

DNA is organized into genes that make up twisty ribbonlike chromosomes. Chromosomes are extremely small, but under a microscope they look like two corkscrew-shaped threads connected by multiple straight rungs, something like a ladder. The rungs are the information-packed genes. The nucleus of a human cell contains forty-six chromosomes in twenty-three identical pairs.

Genes contain information provided by both an individual's mother and father, who most often come from different families. This mixing of genes from different sources makes a person healthier and creates individuals with new and unique characteristics. Inbred offspring—children of people who are closely related—tend to suffer from genetic abnormalities. No one on Earth is exactly like you, unless you have an identical twin, and even then there are slight differences. You may resemble your father, mother, or another relative, but your genetic makeup is entirely your own.

## Mapping the Human Genome

In 1990, the United States Department of Energy and the National Institutes of Health began a thirteen-year series of studies called the Human Genome Project. Amazingly, researchers have identified the approximately 30,000 genes found in human DNA. A working draft of the genes was released in June 2000, with a more detailed analysis released in February 2001. Scientists have also determined the sequence, or order, of many of the billions of individual chemical components that make up human DNA.

The researchers hope to use this information, stored in computer data banks, for medical applications. For example, if the specific genes involved in a disease are identified, it will be easier to find a cure for that disease.

## CELL DIVISION

In addition to basic physical similarities, all cells at some point have the ability to reproduce themselves. This process is called cell division. A cell may copy itself exactly, a process called mitosis, or divide into two "incomplete" germ cells, which is called meiosis.

Mitosis in cells occurs when a fertilized egg in a mother's womb is developing into a fetus, or when cells in certain parts

An artist's conception of how stem cells transform themselves into specialized tissues, both in the body and in the laboratory.

**EMBRYONIC STEM CELLS**
At this stage, scientists can remove stem cells from the inner cell mass. In theory, they can be coaxed to develop into any cell type in the body.

# The Body's Master Builders

Embryonic stem cells, the cells from which all body tissues grow, form about five days after sperm and egg unite, when the embryo is little more than a hollow blastocyst with an inner mass of stem cells. At this stage, researchers can remove these stem cells in hopes of using them to grow re placement tissues to treat a variety of diseases.

## Creating Organs in the Body

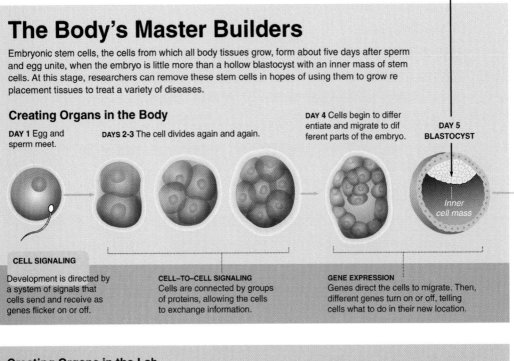

**DAY 1** Egg and sperm meet.

**DAYS 2-3** The cell divides again and again.

**DAY 4** Cells begin to differ entiate and migrate to dif ferent parts of the embryo.

**DAY 5 BLASTOCYST**

*Inner cell mass*

**CELL SIGNALING**
Development is directed by a system of signals that cells send and receive as genes flicker on or off.

**CELL–TO–CELL SIGNALING**
Cells are connected by groups of proteins, allowing the cells to exchange information.

**GENE EXPRESSION**
Genes direct the cells to migrate. Then, different genes turn on or off, telling cells what to do in their new location.

## Creating Organs in the Lab

Biologists at the National Institutes of Health used embryonic stem cells from a mouse blastocyst.

The cells formed clusters showing characteristics of different types of tissue.

Scientists isolated cells that produced a protein common to both the cells of the pancreas and the nervous system.

*Inner cell mass*

**CELL SIGNALING**
Scientists encourage cells to differentiate by exposing them to certain factors (proteins) or tissue types.

**CELL–TO–CELL SIGNALING**
Scientists allow cells to signal each other, and they begin to differentiate.

**GENE EXPRESSION**
When specific genes are active, cells produce certain proteins that scientists can recognize.

Inner
cell
mass

**DAYS 6-9** The embryo im
plants in the uterine wall.

**DAY 14** The inner cell mass gives rise to three cell
layers that will form all the body's tissues and organs.

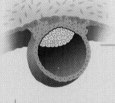

**ECTODERM**
Hair, neuron, skin

**MESODERM**
Heart muscle,
bone, blood

**ENDODERM**
Intestinal lining,
bladder, pancreas

The endoderm is thought to give
rise to specialized stem cells, which
in turn yield all pancreatic cells, in
cluding those that secrete insulin.

**Pancreas**

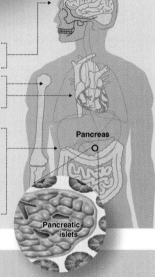

**Pancreatic
islets**

**ENVIRONMENT-SPECIFIC SIGNALING**
As they differentiate, cells receive sig
naling factors from the surrounding
tissues, pushing them to specialize.

The cells were exposed to a growth
signal, and they further differentiated
into precursors to pancreas cells.

**Islet-like
clusters**

Science

The growth signal was withdrawn, and the cells assembled into
insulin-secreting clusters. When inserted into mice, the cells
produced insulin, though not nearly as much as normal, healthy
pancreas cells.

**ENVIRONMENT-SPECIFIC SIGNALING**
Scientists can expedite differentiation
in the lab by exposing cells to signals
they would encounter in the body.

Sources: Dr. Ronald D. G. McKay, Dr. Nadya Lumelsky, National
Institutes of Health; Dr. Nora Sarvetnick, Scripps Research Institute

Steve Duenes; Illustrations by Juan Velasco/The New York Times

13

of an adult's body need to be replaced. During mitosis, the forty-six chromosomes within a cell duplicate themselves, and the duplicated chromosomes then move to opposite sides of the cell. The cytoplasm splits in half, and a new membrane forms around each half. The end result is two new cells identical to the parent cell, with forty-six chromosomes each.

Meiosis occurs only in cells involved in sexual reproduction. During meiosis, the cell splits apart, but the chromosomes do not duplicate themselves. Instead, the identical pairs line up next to each other, and then one full set of twenty-three chromosomes is pulled into each new cell. Such cells are called haploids because they contain only half the chromosomes of a normal cell. Haploids are ready to combine again with other haploids, creating normal diploid cells with a full set of forty-six chromosomes. When, for example, a male sperm cell encounters a female egg cell, the two cells join to form a fertilized cell with a full set of chromosomes, with twenty-three chromosomes from each parent. This splitting and mixing of genetic material is how we inherit genes from both our mothers and fathers.

## DIFFERENCES AMONG CELLS

Although cells divide in a similar way and share the same basic structure, there are many differences among cells.

Some are long and pointy, while others are short and fat. These differences depend on what job the cell must perform. Nerve cells, for example, are long and threadlike. Similar to electrical wires, these cells are designed to transmit impulses containing messages. When you lift a leg, for example, a command from your brain shoots down nerve cells through the spine and into the leg.

Red blood cells are entirely different. They look like miniature doughnuts. This shape enables them to carry oxygen throughout the body and transport carbon dioxide out of cells. Yet another type of cell is found in muscle tissue. Muscle cells are long and contain bundles of fibers. Like rubber bands, they can relax or contract, which allows for movement. Think of how a heart must squeeze each time it pumps. The heart is actually made up of numerous muscle cells.

Given such differences among cells, their extremely small size, and their complex inner structure, you can imagine what a challenge it is for scientists and doctors to replace individual cells and repair damage to them. Until recently, these techniques were considered impractical. Thanks to innovative work with stem cells, however, cell repair and replacement is a possibility within your lifetime.

Dolly *(right)* was the first sheep to be cloned from an adult sheep. With her is Polly, who was cloned with an extra human gene.

# 2 ▷ Stem Cells

A stem cell is very much like most other cells. It has a membrane, cytoplasm, and other attributes associated with cells. It also can divide and duplicate itself, an ability that other cells possess. There are, however, some things about a stem cell that make it very special. Stem cells can divide indefinitely. Also, they are not specialized, like cells that can only work as heart muscle, for example. With proper care and coaxing, stem cells can transform themselves into any type of cell.

## A COPY MACHINE THAT NEVER QUITS

Virtually all cells at some point divide and reproduce themselves. This in itself is a miraculous feat. Imagine if you could step into a machine and make carbon copies of yourself. That's what cells do every day. While scientists have duplicated the process by cloning animals, such as Dolly the sheep, cloning is still complicated and controversial. With cells, copying is a piece of cake. In fact, this happens in your body every day. For example, you might have suffered a bad sunburn that caused your skin to peel, or a cut that left a mark on your skin. Over time, these minor injuries usually heal themselves, as skin cells reproduce and make new skin.

Most cells are limited in their ability to duplicate. This is especially true when a cell is taken outside of a living human or animal and is maintained in a laboratory setting. Cells in a living organism are called in vivo, which is Latin for "in the living." Cells kept alive outside of a body in a lab setting are called in vitro, which means "in glass" in Latin. This refers to the fact that the cells are housed in an artificial enclosure, usually a glass dish or test tube.

If the conditions are right, stem cells have the ability to copy themselves indefinitely. Scientists hope to grow large masses of stem

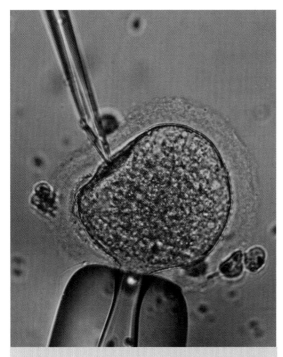

A human egg cell fertilized in a test tube, a procedure called in vitro fertilization

cell tissue in laboratories. They hope that in the future, with the help of stem cells, humans will be able to repair worn-out parts of the body as easily as they now repair a damaged part of a car or computer.

## CELLS WITH ENDLESS POTENTIAL

Again, stem cells are unspecialized cells. They do not carry out specific functions, as do other cells. For example, neurons, or nerve cells, work only in the nervous system. Epithelia, or skin cells, are unique to the skin. Most stem cells are like notebooks filled with empty pages. Just as a person can create a book by writing on blank pieces of paper, scientists hope to turn blank stem cells into whatever kind of cells they need.

Stem cells are like people who have not decided what they want to do when they grow up. Education and experience can help a person make that decision. In the case of stem cells, researchers can coax the cells to become certain types of specialized cells by changing their environment in the lab. For example, scientists can alter the food and growing medium in the container holding the stem cells. A lot of scientific work is still needed before we can create made-to-order cell types for the more than 200 kinds of human cells, but current research strongly suggests that this will be a future possibility.

Fertilization occurs when a sperm cell enters an egg cell and unites with it.

# Embryonic Stem Cells

Stem cells are classified into three basic categories, depending on where and how scientists obtain the cells. The first type is called an embryonic stem cell. The word "embryonic" refers to an embryo, an immature organism in the first days of its development. Embryonic stem cells, therefore, come from an embryo.

## REPRODUCTION

The growth and development of an embryo before birth, or gestation, begins right after conception, when a male sperm unites with a female egg. The sperm contains an enzyme that breaks down the outer surface of the egg cell. This enables the sperm to enter the egg. The egg and sperm cells then join to form a single nucleus. At this point the egg is fertilized and ready to grow into an embryo.

A fertilized human egg is programmed to divide over and over again until, after one to five days, it forms a round ball of cells called a blastocyst. A blastocyst under a microscope basically looks like a soap bubble filled with liquid, with a bunch of egg-shaped smaller

## Cloning

A clone is a living organism that has exactly the same genetic makeup as another plant or animal. Human clones are probably more common than you think, with identical twins having the same genes.

Cloning received a lot of attention in 1996, when scientists artificially cloned a sheep named Dolly by destroying the nucleus of the mother sheep's egg cell and inserting a nucleus obtained from another sheep. Since that time, scientists have cloned other animals, such as mice and cattle. The merits of artificial human cloning are, however, hotly debated. For now, unless you have an identical twin, your genetic structure is yours and yours alone.

cells gathered into one corner of the bubble. These smaller cells are the embryonic stem cells.

When the blastocyst containing the embryonic stem cells is approximately two days old, the stem cells are totipotent. This means that they have the potential of forming an entire human being. When the blastocyst is about four days old, the stem cells within it are said to be pluripotent. This means that they can now divide and turn into any type of cell within the body. At eight days old, the cells have become more specialized and are now called multipotent. At this stage they begin to form any of the numerous types of cells, such as nerve or muscle cells, that make up a person. Eventually, multipotent stem cells will begin to clump together to form actual organs. For example, heart muscle cells will turn into a heart and cartilage cells will begin to form the first stages of a skeleton.

## THE IMPORTANCE OF PLURIPOTENCE

Scientists are most interested in the middle stage of blastocyst development, when the embryonic stem cells are pluripotent. Think of these cells as clay. At first, most clay is wet and easy to work with. After a while it begins to harden, but it can still be pushed into different shapes and figures. If enough time passes, the clay hardens and is no longer malleable.

Human blastocysts

When embryonic stem cells reach the pluripotent stage, scientists remove them from the blastocyst and transfer them to a petri dish, a flat, round glass dish used in laboratories. Like chefs, the scientists can then add various chemical recipes to direct the growth of the cells. Eventually, researchers hope to be able to create in the laboratory each of the more than 200 types of cells found within the human body.

## EMBRYOS FOR SCIENTIFIC RESEARCH

For many years, scientists have studied the embryos of mice in the laboratory. Stem cells from these embryos, however, cannot by themselves form human cells. Researchers next turned to human embryos obtained from in vitro fertilization clinics. Couples who have trouble conceiving a child often turn to such clinics for help.

At the clinic, doctors collect eggs from the mother and sperm from the father. They then fertilize the eggs outside of the body and surgically implant them into the mother's womb. To ensure that the process is successful, the doctors usually fertilize more than one egg. The extra embryos are put into a storage freezer, in case the first fertilized egg does not grow properly. The scientists who originally worked with embryonic stem cells obtained embryos from these stored extras, which are otherwise thrown away.

## CELL LINES

Since stem cells can divide and copy themselves over and over again, researchers can maintain a stock of living embryonic stem cells without always having to obtain them from a human embryo. The resulting stock is called a cell line. It is similar to your family lineage. You are at the end of a long line of ancestors who lived before you. Similarly, embryonic stem cells are descended from lines that can go back to the original master cells taken from an embryo. Many scientists believe that it is not always safe to work with stem cells from older cell lines, as problems can occur as time goes on. However, because of the controversy surrounding the use of human embryos in research, many scientists choose to work with the existing cell lines.

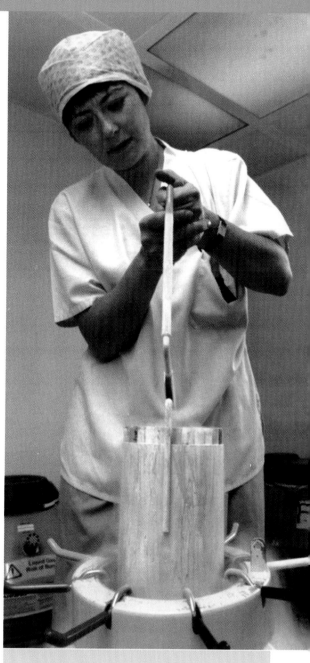

A scientist displays a cylinder containing frozen human embryos.

A twenty-week-old fetus. As the fetus develops, undifferentiated stem cells transform themselves into nerve cells, blood cells, muscle cells, and other tissues.

# ◆ 4 ◆ Embryonic Germ Cells

The second type of stem cell is called an embryonic germ cell. Germ cells are the reproductive cells that form sperm or eggs. Embryonic germ cells, therefore, refer to stem cells that come from sperm and eggs and that are designed to combine to produce an embryo.

Embryonic germ cells are obtained from a human fetus. The word "fetus" is used to describe a developing organism that is older and more developed than an embryo, though still at a stage before birth. An embryo is like a plant seed with a few tiny roots on it. A fetus is comparable to a plant seed that has already grown a small shoot and may in a crude way resemble the adult plant. Scientists obtain these stem cells from five- to ten-week-old fetuses.

## PASSING THE STEM CELL TEST

Scientists look for certain qualities in stem cells. These attributes ensure that the cell will be useful in research. You might do a similar thing when choosing teammates for sports. Let's say you need to find friends for a game of football. You might look for someone who can run fast, kick accurately, and perform other skills required of the game. Similarly, researchers seek out cells that will be helpful in scientific studies.

Both embryonic germ cells and embryonic stem cells must pass certain tests to make sure they are fit for research. In a lab, these cells must show that they can copy themselves for long periods of time. Like a copy machine that does not shut off, they must keep dividing and replicating indefinitely, as long as they are cared for properly.

Embryonic germ cells and embryonic stem cells must also have no chromosome abnormalities. Remember that chromosomes are like computer programs. They contain important information about who we are. A genetic abnormality is just like a bug in a computer program that will prevent the program from working properly. Cells grown from stem cells with defective chromosomes will not function the way they should. They may even die.

The final test is whether or not the cells are pluripotent—that is, able to transform into different cell types. Ideally, a stem cell can turn into each of three basic cell forms: endoderm, mesoderm, and ectoderm. Endoderm cells over time produce the lungs, the digestive system, and other inner organs. Mesoderm cells eventually produce bone, muscle, and connective tissue. Ectoderm cells turn into the brain, nerves, and skin. Both embryonic germ cells and embryonic stem cells can give rise to these three groups if they have reached pluripotency.

## IMPORTANCE OF THE TEST

Why must these stem cells undergo such rigorous testing? Consider what might happen if a stem cell had a bad chromosome. A person receiving that cell could

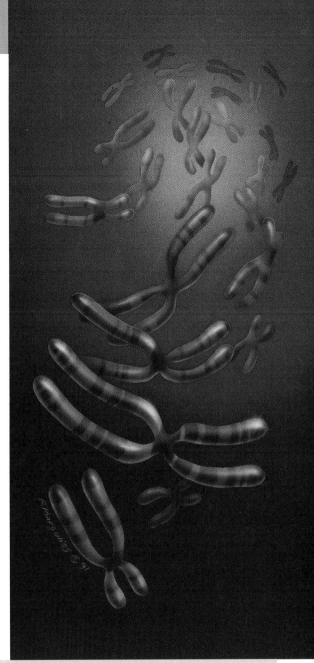

Human cells normally have twenty-three pairs of threadlike chromosomes that contain DNA. Chromosomes can be seen, after being stained with a dye, through powerful microscopes.

# Rules for Testing

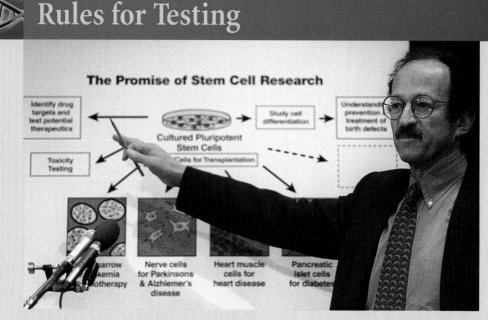

Director of the National Institutes of Health, Dr. Harold Varmus, discusses stem cell research during a congressional hearing.

When you take a test in school, there are certain rules that must be followed. The teacher may ask that you not talk or leave your seat without first obtaining permission. Scientists performing stem cell research also must follow certain rules.

In the United States, the National Institutes of Health (NIH) establishes standards for all medical research facilities that receive funding from the federal government. Stem cell work is expensive, so federal money is greatly desired. Different rules, however, apply for privately funded laboratories, which do not fall under the authority of the NIH.

develop a serious medical condition. If the cells are defective so that they cannot divide over and over again, researchers would not be able to maintain them in a lab. In a way, stem cell researchers are like farmers with cells as their crop, and they must maintain high-quality seed. The exception to this is the use of embryonic germ cells from embryos and fetuses. These are like first-generation seeds and are much more likely to be free of genetic defects. But such cells, as we have said, are hard to obtain and their use is controversial.

It is necessary for scientists to learn the mechanism by which stem cells turn into the three basic cell forms before much progress in biomedical research can be made. Let's say that a stem cell can produce only nerve cells. This would not provide much help for someone who has suffered heart damage and needs muscle cells for their heart. The complex biological and chemical processes that trigger the development of one cell type instead of another need to be understood.

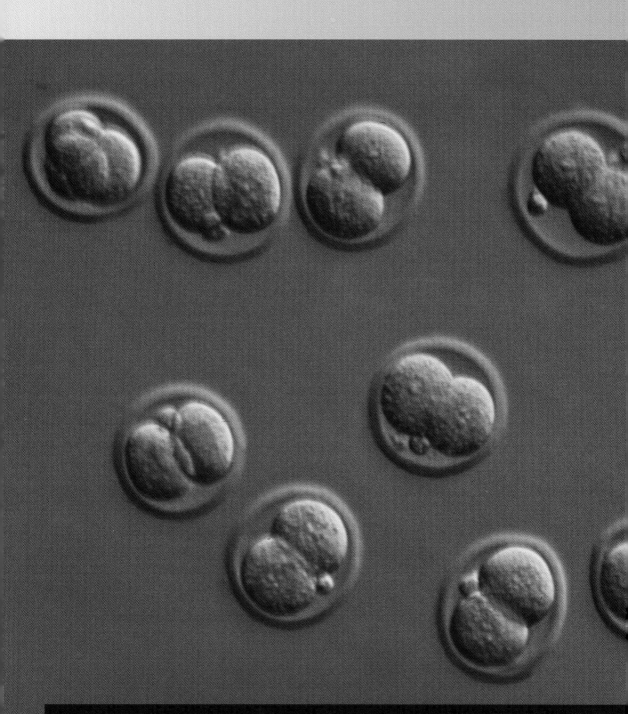

Two-celled human embryos photographed shortly after fertilization. Such embryos are one source of stem cells, but stem cells can also be found in adult humans.

# 5

# Adult Stem Cells

The third and final type of stem cell is the adult stem cell. The word "adult" refers to where these cells are found and to their age. Adult stem cells are extracted from fully formed humans, like you. Embryonic stem cells and embryonic germ cells, on the other hand, are obtained from embryos and fetuses that have not yet fully developed into people. "Adult" also applies to the age of these cells. They are more mature and set in their ways than the other two types of stem cells.

Think of a puppy compared to a full-grown dog. The puppy is energetic and easygoing. You can train it to do all kinds of things, from catching balls to sitting on command. While older dogs can learn new things, it is harder for them to adjust to new habits. If you take an older dog for a walk at a certain time for a number of days, it is going to want to walk at that time every day.

Adult stem cells, like older dogs and people, are harder to change. They are programmed to work a certain way and always want to follow a certain routine. This makes it harder for scientists to coax them, with different chemicals and growing mediums, into various types of specialized cells. Despite the problems, adult stem cells show remarkable promise for future medicine.

## FINDING ADULT STEM CELLS

Embryonic stem cells and embryonic germ cells are found only in specific locations in the developing embryo. Embryonic stem cells, for example, are located in the little clump of cells within the blastocyst and in no other area. Embryonic germ cells are found only in one region of the fetus. Adult stem cells, on the other hand, are virtually everywhere in the body.

Researchers have found adult stem cells in bone marrow, the soft red material that lies in the center of bones. Bone marrow is essential to good health. It is here that red blood cells, virus-fighting white blood cells, and other essential components of blood are created. Adult stem cells have also been found within blood itself.

Although you cannot see them, adult stem cells are also in your eyes. Specifically, they are found in the cornea and in the retina. The cornea is the clear outer part of the eye. It is what gives eyes their glassy look. The retina is located at the back of the eye. It is where eyes begin to turn reflected light into images, sort of like the film in a camera.

Many other parts of the body contain adult stem cells. These include the brain, skeletal muscles, liver, skin, digestive tract, and pancreas, which is the organ that produces digestive juices and a chemical called insulin that helps process sugars. Adult stem cells have even been found in the mouth. There they are located within dental pulp. Although teeth feel like solid objects, the hard enamel on the outside of each tooth is really just a shell encasing soft pulp at the bottom of the tooth.

## HOW ADULT STEM CELLS WORK

Like embryonic stem cells, adult stem cells are not specialized. They are ready to develop into whatever cell is needed by the organ or body part in which they are housed. Because they are located within a specific part of the body, they tend to work only in that area. For example, a cornea or retina stem cell can copy itself to repair parts of the eye. Scientists refer to the copying ability of adult stem cells as self-renewal. These cells can make identical copies of themselves for as long as the person or organism lives.

The copying ability of adult stem cells is a bit more complicated than that of embryonic stem and germ cells. Instead of just churning out copies one after another, the adult stem cell produces a middleman of sorts, called a precursor cell, which matures into the copy. Let's say that an adult stem cell in the brain is ready to divide. It would first create a precursor cell. The precursor would then develop the characteristics associated with a specific cell type, such as a nerve cell, with its long and thin structure.

## AN IMPORTANT DISCOVERY

In recent years, scientists have discovered that adult stem cells are not limited to just making the types of mature cells found within their surrounding tissue. Studies suggest that adult stem cells can produce all kinds of different specialized cells. For example, adult stem cells in the brain can be coaxed to make blood cells in a laboratory setting. Adult stem cells in bone marrow appear to be able to produce skeletal muscles and liver cells. Adult stem cells' ability to transform themselves into different types of cells is called plasticity. The term "plasticity" means that these cells appear to be able to mold themselves into various types of cells with different shapes and sizes.

## ADULT STEM CELL BENEFITS

One of the concerns surrounding the use of stem cell therapy—the insertion of stem cells into damaged parts of the body—is that the person receiving them could have an adverse reaction. The immune system, sensing that something foreign has entered the body, could attack the cells. Normally

## A Mystery Surrounding Adult Stem Cells

While scientists know that adult stem cells exist, they do not know what their source is. It is easy to answer this question for embryonic stem cells and embryonic germ cells because researchers can see how they emerge and develop from embryonic tissue. With adult stem cells, no one really knows much about their source, although there are a couple of theories.

Some researchers believe that adult stem cells may be leftover embryonic stem cells, going back to the embryonic development of the individual in the womb. Another theory is that adult stem cells arise during some other phase of human development. Right now, most studies tend to support this second theory, but the answer remains an unsolved mystery.

this immune reaction helps people. When a flu bug enters the body and the immune system attacks it, the immune system is doing what it is supposed to do. The immune system, however, may not know the difference between a dangerous germ and a helpful stem cell from an outside source.

Adult stem cells can eliminate the problem of an adverse immune system reaction because they can come from the individual's own body. The immune system, therefore, is not likely to reject them.

Another advantage is that research on adult stem cells is far less controversial than research on stem cells derived from embryos and fetuses. For religious, moral, or political reasons, some people do not approve of embryonic stem cell and embryonic germ cell studies. Most people, however, do not have ethical concerns about scientific work on adult stem cells.

## ADULT STEM CELL DISADVANTAGES

The bad news is that researchers face a number of challenges when studying adult stem cells. First of all, adult stem cells play a sort of hide-and-seek game. They are hidden away in certain parts of the body, so scientists have the challenge of trying to find them. Imagine having to search through billions of cells just to find one adult stem cell. That is what often happens.

Another problem with adult stem cells is that, because they are more mature and set in their ways, they are not as flexible as embryonic stem cells. While adult stem cells have a certain amount of plasticity, it appears that they can make only certain other types of cells, instead of all of the over 200 types that exist. As a result, they may only be able to cure a

Antiabortion activist Randall Terry, founder of Operation Rescue, at a demonstration in front of the White House in 2001 urging President Bush to ban stem cell research.

handful of diseases. Embryonic stem cells, however, have the potential of curing countless diseases.

Yet another problem is that adult stem cells grow very slowly and seem to have a limited life span when grown in vitro in a laboratory. It can take months for researchers to transform an adult stem cell into a desired cell type. If a person is very ill, the wait may be too long and the patient could die.

Despite such disadvantages, research continues on adult stem cells. As techniques in developing and maintaining them improve, so do the chances that these cells will one day be widely used to treat many different conditions and diseases.

Louise Brown *(center)*, the world's first test-tube baby, with her parents

# 6

# The History of Stem Cell Research

The science of cytology, or the study of cells, began hundreds of years ago. In 1665, an English physicist named Robert Hooke wrote what is believed to be the first description of cells. With the advent of microscopes, German botanist Matthias Jakob Schleiden in 1838 theorized that all living organisms are made up of cells. He was right!

While scientists have known about cells for a long time, stem cell research is a relatively new field of study. In fact, if you look at science textbooks published even up to the mid-1990s, you will probably find little if any information on stem cells.

Initial work began in the late 1800s, when doctors began to try to fertilize eggs from mammals in a laboratory setting. The first attempt was documented in the year 1878. At this point, scientists were experimenting only on animals and not humans.

## RESEARCH THROUGH THE 1970s

In the decades that followed after the late 1800s, scientists repeatedly tried to fertilize eggs in vitro

Because mammalian eggs are small and hard to work with in a lab, the researchers did not have much luck. In 1959, however, there was a breakthrough. Scientists produced rabbits using in vitro fertilization. More rabbits was not the real goal. In vitro fertilization of human eggs was.

Another step toward this goal was made during the early to mid-1960s. Studies on mice revealed that certain cells found in their sexual organs could produce many different kinds of cells. This really was the first time researchers began to think about stem cells as blank cells that could be transformed into various cell types. In 1968, two researchers successfully fertilized a human egg in vitro. Human births as a result of in vitro fertilization did not occur until ten years later.

## RESEARCH IN THE 1980s

During the 1980s, scientists continued to improve in vitro fertilization techniques. In 1981, the first baby conceived with this technique in the United States, Elizabeth Carr, was born. She was the third in vitro baby worldwide, following earlier similar births in England and Australia.

In addition to laboratory work concerning human conception, scientists continued to study cells derived from animals. In 1981, embryonic stem cells were taken from mouse blastocysts. Scientists put these cells through a number of

## The Evolution of Microscopes

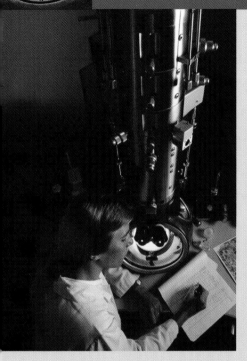

An electron microscope

Since cells are so tiny, it would be impossible to study them without the use of powerful microscopes. Early microscopes resembled simple magnifying glasses and were not very strong. This limited research on cells.

Stronger microscopes began to be developed in the late 1800s, which revived interest in cell research. By the twentieth century, all kinds of powerful microscopes had been invented. These included X-ray microscopes and electron microscopes. As a result, scientists can get a better look at cells and stem cells.

tests to see if they had the plasticity to produce the three basic types of cells found in mammals, and also to show that they were structured in a normal way, with regular membranes and other features associated with cells.

In the mid-1980s, a team of scientists worked for over three years on a study involving cells taken from the testicles of a human male. The scientists were able to clone the cells, producing identical copies. They were also able to turn them into neurons and other types of cells after exposing them to a special kind of acid.

By 1989, yet another group of scientists was able to clone cells taken from a human embryo. While these were not technically stem cells, they did show how young cells in a developing human embryo could turn into tissue made up of the three basic types of cells. At this stage, scientists were still struggling to keep the cells extracted from the embryo alive and dividing in the lab. Also, the cells in the lab had abnormal numbers of chromosomes. The research was promising, but problematic.

## STEM CELL RESEARCH IN THE 1990s

In 1994, researchers had more success in working with cells extracted from human blastocysts. Scientists could now obtain cells with normal numbers of chromosomes in the laboratory. They could also make the cells live longer.

In 1995 and 1996, great success was achieved in studying stem cells taken from the embryos of rhesus monkeys and marmosets, two primates that are very closely related to humans. The problems experienced in the previous cell studies were worked out. Researchers concluded that it should be possible to work just as easily with embryonic human cells.

The year 1998 proved to be the golden year in terms of stem cell research. Two very important studies occurred that year. In the first, a University of Wisconsin team of scientists isolated embryonic stem cells from a human blastocyst. The cells passed all of the tests. They divided repeatedly in the lab, they retained characteristics associated with normal cells, and they were able to produce the three basic cell types.

That same year, at around the same exact time, a team of researchers from Johns Hopkins Medical Institutions derived embryonic germ cells from a human fetus. While the University of Wisconsin study produced cells that were definitely pluripotent, the Johns Hopkins' scientists could not definitively prove the pluripotence of their embryonic germ cells. Still, certain chemical indicators suggested that these fetal cells could turn into the three primary cell types.

## STEM CELL RESEARCH AFTER 1998

Since the discoveries of 1998, there has been increased interest in stem cell research. In 2001, organizations such as the National Institutes of Health forecast what such research could lead to. Their predictions include possible treatments for a number of diseases and the hope that stem cells could be used to grow human tissues, such as heart muscle cells, in the laboratory.

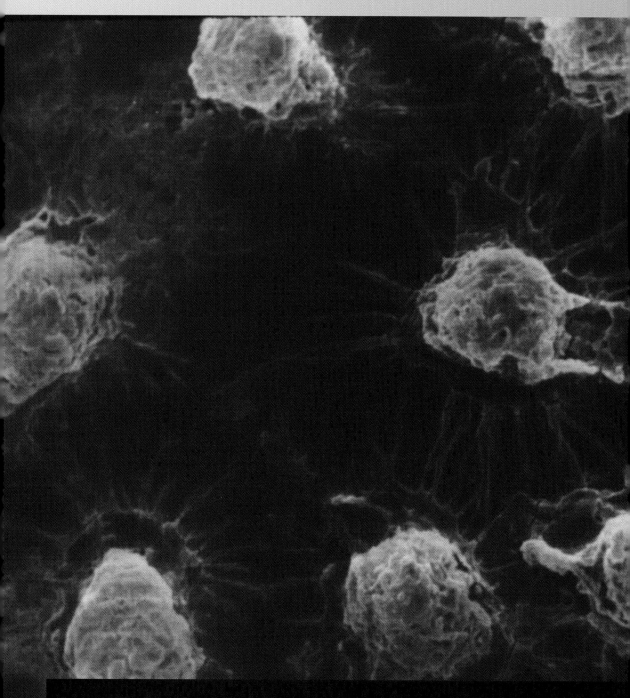

Stem cells from bone marrow migrate to the bloodstream, where they will form lymphocytes.

# 7

# How Stem Cells Are Now Being Used

Right now, stem cells are being used in three ways. First, researchers continue to study them in the laboratory, hoping to further understand how they work and to ensure their safe use. Second, stem cells are already being tested in humans with serious medical conditions. Third, a special type of stem cell, called hematopoietic, is now being used to save lives.

## PROMISING STUDIES

Successful stem cell work on animals often leads to human benefits. For example, think of how the researchers who studied embryonic monkey and marmoset stem cells predicted that similar work on human embryonic stem cells would soon follow. Sure enough, it took only a few years for scientists to perform comparable studies using human embryos.

Some of the most promising work concerning stem cells involves restoring movement to paralyzed people. Because of birth defects, accidents, or

Actor Christopher Reeves, who became popular for playing Superman, testifies at a Senate hearing on stem cell research in 2000. Reeves was paralyzed from the neck down in a horse-riding accident in 1995.

disease, paralyzed individuals lose the ability to move one or more limbs. Generally what happens is that signals from neurons, or nerve cells, leading from the spinal cord can no longer send messages to muscles in the limbs. It would be like cutting one of the cables on a computer.

In the past, people who became paralyzed had little hope of recovering limb function. Researchers in 2000, however, restored movement to paralyzed mice and rats by injecting stem cells into the fluid within the rodents' spines. The stem cells began to divide and, by themselves, turned into nerve cells. Just a few injected stem cells made a big difference in the health of the rodents. The study suggests that one day a similar therapy could be used to treat paralyzed humans.

## STUDIES ON HUMANS

Parkinson's disease is a debilitating condition that affects certain nerve cells in the brain. When these cells are working properly, they release a chemical called dopamine that helps transmit nerve signals. When the cells are not working as they should, a person does not have complete control over his or her movements. Such people can have slight tremors or may have trouble picking up objects or walking. While more research is needed, scientists have had some success in implanting stem cells into the brains of Parkinson's patients. These stem cells often divide and develop into functioning nerve cells that release the proper amounts of dopamine.

People with other serious diseases also have undergone successful stem cell therapies. Because the treatments involve certain risks at this point, such as complications from brain surgery in treating Parkinson's, scientists hope to soon come up with less risky and invasive procedures involving stem cells.

## Cord Blood Banks

You may have heard the term "blood bank." It refers to places where human blood is collected and stored. Stem cell research has led to a new kind of bank called a cord blood bank. Here, hematopoietic stem cells from placentas and umbilical cords are stored. For a fee, some banks even allow parents to store their child's cord blood cells when the child is born, just in case he or she develops a serious illness at a later time.

# HEMATOPOIETIC STEM CELLS

One type of embryonic stem cell, called a hematopoietic stem cell, is already being used to treat sick children. Hematopoietic stem cells come from the placentas and umbilical cords of newborn babies. The placenta is tissue that enables food and oxygen to nourish a baby when it is still in its mother's womb. The umbilical cord carries the food and oxygen from the mother to the baby.

Hematopoietic stem cells are precursors to blood cells, so they can divide and make red blood cells, germ-fighting white blood cells, and platelets that help blood to clot. Children with immune deficiencies or blood-related

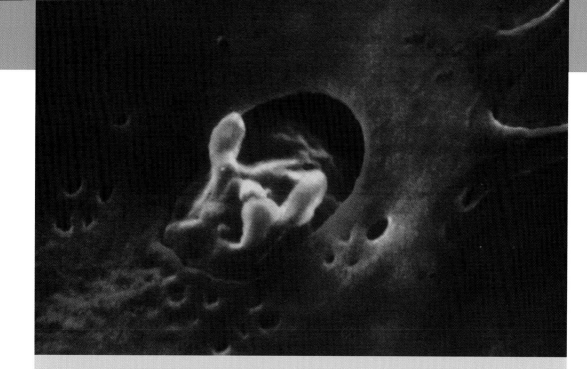

This microscopic image shows white blood cells migrating from bone marrow, where they mature, to the lumen of a blood vessel. White blood cells fight against germs and viruses in the human body.

diseases, such as leukemia, in which white blood cells divide abnormally, can benefit from hematopoietic stem cells. When these cells are injected into a sick child, they often help to restore that patient's immune system. The stem cells divide to form normal blood cells that replace the ones that have been damaged by disease.

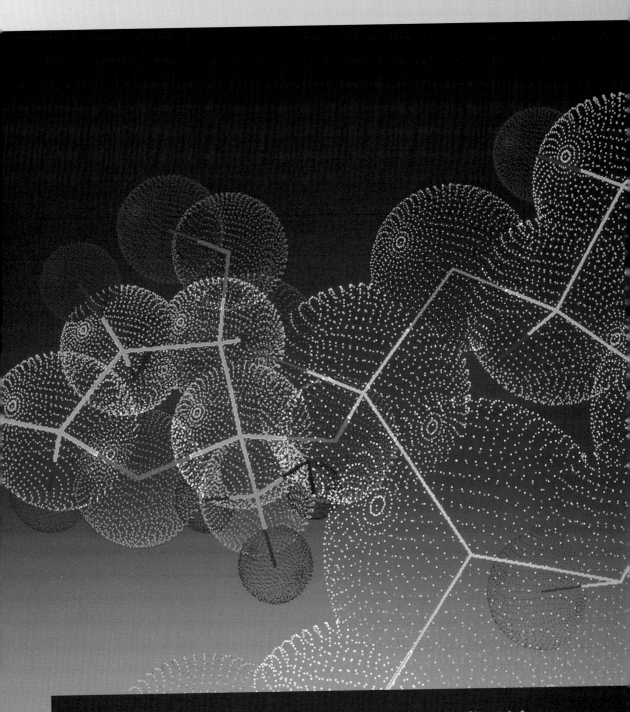

An electron micrograph of crystals of the hormone insulin. Diabetes is caused by a lack of this hormone in the body.

# 8 Future Treatments Using Stem Cells

In the near future, cures and treatments for many diseases may be possible because of stem cell research. In addition to promising help for patients suffering from paralysis and Parkinson's disease, researchers are hopeful that individuals affected by diabetes, heart disease, genetic diseases, and cancer may soon benefit

## DIABETES

Diabetes is a disease that affects many people worldwide. At first it leads to excessive thirst and weight loss, but complications can be serious and may lead to blindness and circulatory disorders. Diabetes is caused by the lack of a hormone called insulin. Insulin is produced in an organ called the pancreas. This hormone lowers the level of sugar in the blood. Sugar is present in many foods, but too much of it is not good for you. The pancreas of a person with diabetes does not produce enough insulin. People with diabetes, therefore, often have to have daily injections of insulin. This helps their condition but does not cure it.

## Stem Cells as Surrogate Humans

When scientists discover a new drug or come up with a new product, such as shampoo, they often must first test it on animals and then on humans to determine if it is safe. The process can be risky, expensive, and controversial. Many people, for example, do not believe that animals should be subjected to such testing, especially for developing shampoo or other beauty products.

In the future, scientists may be able to test different chemical combinations on tissue created from stem cells. This would ensure that the testing would not directly hurt animals or humans. The cost would also be minimal, as stem cells can reproduce themselves indefinitely under the right conditions.

Doctors may one day be able to inject stem cells into the pancreas of a person with diabetes. The stem cells could divide and produce healthy pancreatic cells that would produce the proper amount of insulin. This could end the need for daily injections, and it might get rid of the disease altogether.

## HEART DISEASE

Heart disease leads to many deaths each year. Probably a member of your own immediate or extended family has at

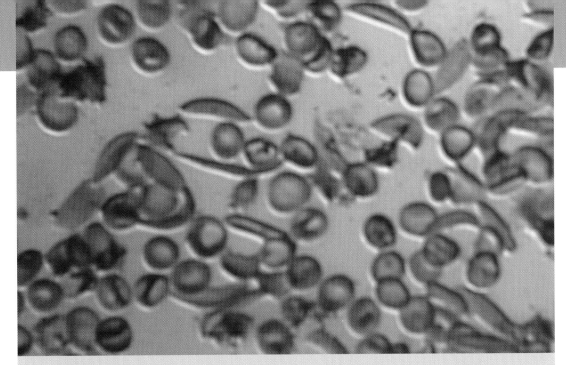

Deformed red blood cells can be seen in this sample taken from someone suffering from sickle-cell anemia. Researchers hope that stem cells can be used to treat such genetic diseases.

some point either suffered a heart attack or died as a result of heart disease. Often, after a heart attack or serious illness involving the heart, cells in the heart become damaged and die. The heart then does not work properly. Researchers hope to transform stem cells into heart muscle cells that could replace the damaged ones.

## GENETIC DISEASE

Some people are born with genetic defects that can cause serious health problems. Because these problems often occur at birth, they hit children especially hard. Examples of genetic diseases include Down syndrome, cystic fibrosis, and sickle-cell anemia. Researchers hope that in the future stem cells without defects can be used to cure genetic diseases.

# CANCER

Stem cells could help treat cancer patients in at least three ways. First, patients who have suffered damage to their immune systems after treatments like chemotherapy and radiation may be able to have their immune systems restored with stem cells. Second, stem cells might be used to replace diseased or damaged tissue. Finally, researchers are hoping to create cancer-killing cells out of stem cells that can literally eat away and destroy cancer.

Stem cell research is still in its infancy, but already promising strides have been made in finding treatments and cures for diseases like cancer and Parkinson's. Thanks to stem cell discoveries, many medical breakthroughs are within reach. Stem cells may one day save your life, and the lives of future generations.

# Glossary

**adult stem cell**  A cell found throughout the human body that can divide and turn into different types of cells.

**blastocyst**  One of the earliest stages of gestation; a small sphere containing fluid and a group of small cells. These are embryonic stem cells.

**cell**  The basic building block, or structural unit, of all plants and animals, including humans.

**cell division**  The process by which a cell splits in half to create two new cells.

**cell line**  A line of descent from an original source. In the same way that people have a family tree, cells have a family lineage that can be traced back in time.

**chromosomes**  Ribbonlike structures consisting of genes made out of DNA that are found in the nucleus of a cell. They carry inherited information about a person.

**clone**  A living organism that has exactly the same genetic makeup as another plant or animal. Identical twins are the only naturally occurring type of human clone.

**cytoplasm**  The gelatinlike fluid within cells.

**DNA**  The abbreviation for deoxyribonucleic acid, the chemical found within the genes of chromosomes that helps determine a person's traits.

**ectoderm**  An early type of cell found within the embryo that eventually develops into cells that form the brain, nerves, and skin.

**embryo**  The organism that develops after a male sperm has fertilized a female egg.

**embryonic germ cells**  Stem cells derived from fetuses.

**embryonic stem cells**  Stem cells derived from embryos.

**endoderm**  An early type of cell found within the embryo that eventually develops into cells that form the digestive system and the lungs.

**fertilization**  The union of a male sperm and a female egg.

**fetus**  Unborn organism from about eight weeks after fertilization until before birth.

**genes**  Segments, or pieces, of DNA that make up chromosomes.

**hematopoietic stem cell**  A cell that can turn into any of the cells found in blood. This includes red blood cells, white blood cells, and platelets.

**in vitro**  Meaning "in glass"; refers to cells or organisms that are artificially maintained in a laboratory.

**in vitro fertilization**  The union of a sperm and an egg outside the body in a laboratory setting.

**in vivo**  Meaning "in the living"; used to describe living things in their natural environment, such as stem cells that are in the body instead of being developed in a laboratory.

**mesoderm**  An early type of cell found within the embryo that eventually develops into cells that form bone, connective tissue, and muscle.

**plasticity**  The ability of a stem cell to turn into different types of cells.

**pluripotent**  Having the ability to turn into all three basic types of cells: ectoderm, endoderm, and mesoderm.

# For More Information

## ORGANIZATIONS

American Diabetes Association
1701 North Beauregard Street
Alexandria, VA 22311
(800) DIABETES (342-2383)
Web site: http://www.diabetes.org
Research, information, and advocacy concerning diabetes.

National Institutes of Health
Bethesda, MD 20892
Web site: http://www.nih.gov
Offers publications and fact sheets concerning the latest
  innovations in stem cell research.

## WEB SITES

Due to the changing nature of Internet links, the Rosen
Publishing Group, Inc., has developed an online list of
Web sites related to the subject of this book. This site is
updated regularly. Please use this link to access the list:

http://www.rosenlinks.com/lfm/stcr/

# For Further Reading

Baeuerle, Patrick. *The Cell Works* (Microexplorers). Hauppauge, NY: Barron's Educational Series, 1997.

Baeuerle, Patrick. *How the Y Makes the Guy* (Microexplorers). Hauppauge, NY: Barron's Educational Series, 1997.

Baeuerle, Patrick. *Ingenious Genes* (Microexplorers). Hauppauge, NY: Barron's Educational Series, 1997.

DuPrau, Jeanne. *Cells*. San Diego: Kidhaven Press, 2001.

Ganeri, Anita. *Cells and Systems*. Portsmouth, NH: Heinemann Library, 2000.

Handwerker, Mark. *Ready-to-Use Human Biology and Health Activities for Grades 5-12*. Upper Saddle River, NJ: Prentice Hall PTR, 2000.

HarperCollins World Publishing, eds. *Amazing Schemes Within Your Genes*. New York: HarperCollins Publishers, Inc., 1993.

Marshall, Elizabeth. *The Human Genome Project: Cracking the Code Within Us*. Danbury, CT: Franklin Watts, 1997.

Nicholson, Cynthia. *Baa! The Most Interesting Book You'll Ever Read About Genes and Cloning*. Toronto, ON: Kids Can Press Limited, 1999.

Roca, Nuria Bosch. *Cells, Genes, and Chromosomes*. Broomall, PA: Chelsea House Publishers, 1995.

# Bibliography

Chapman, Audrey, et al. *Stem Cell Research and Applications: Monitoring the Frontiers of Biomedical Research.* San Francisco: American Association for the Advancement of Science and Institute for Civil Society, 1999.

Devitt, Terry. Embryonic Stem Cells: Research at the University of Wisconsin at Madison. Retrieved September 2001 (http://www.news.wisc.edu/packages/stemcells).

Firpo, Meri. "Stem Cell." World Book Online Americas Edition. Retrieved September 2001 (http://www.aolsvc.worldbook.aol.com/wbol/wbPage/na/ar/co/726778).

Johns Hopkins University School of Medicine. Press Reports for 2001. Retrieved September 2001 (http://www.med.jhu.edu).

Tenenbaum, David. "Finally, Generic Human Cells Discovered." Retrieved September 2001 (http://whyfiles.org/shorties/stem_cell.html).

University of Wisconsin at Madison. University Communications—Stem Cell Press Kit. Retrieved September 2001 (http://www.news.wisc.edu).

U. S. Department of Health and Human Services. National Institutes of Health. "Stem Cells: Scientific Progress and Future Research Directions." Retrieved September 2001 (http://www.nih.gov/news/stemcell/scireport.htm).

# Index

# Credits

## ABOUT THE AUTHOR

Jennifer Viegas is a reporter for *Discovery News* and is a features columnist for Knight Ridder Newspapers. She also writes for ABC News, Physicians for Social Responsibility, the *Washington Post*, and other publications.

## PHOTO CREDITS

Cover © Dr. Yorgos Nikas/Science Photo Library; cover inset (front and back), p. 1 © PhotoDisc, Getty Images; folio banners © Eyewire; pp. 4–5, 18, 23, 32–33 © Richard G. Rawlins, Ph.D./Custom Medical Stock Photo; pp. 6–7 © J. L. Carson/CMSP; p. 9 © Articulate Graphics/CMSP; pp. 12–13 © Juan Velasco/NYT Graphics; pp. 16–17 © John Chadwick/AP Wide World Photos; pp. 20–21 © Bryson Biomedical Illustrations/CMSP; p. 25 © Findlay Kember/AP Wide World Photos; pp. 26–27 © Keith/CMSP; p. 29 © R. Margulies/CMSP; p. 30 © AFP/Corbis; p. 39 © Stephen J. Boitano/AP Wide World Photos; pp. 40–41 © Adrian Arbib/Corbis; p. 43 © Bob Krist/Corbis; pp. 46–47 © Hossler, Ph.D./CMSP; p. 48 © Reuters NewMedia Inc./Corbis; p. 51 © R. Becker/CMSP; pp. 52–53 © Alfred Pasieka/Science Photo Library; p. 55 © Phil A. Harrington/Peter Arnold, Inc.

## DESIGN AND LAYOUT

Evelyn Horovicz